S0-BXE-233

TO: _____

FROM: _____

# THIS IS YOUR DAY.

IT'S FOR CELEBRATING YOU, YOUR SPIRIT, AND EVERYTHING YOU BRING TO THE WORLD. IT'S ALSO A DAY FOR HAPPINESS AND SMILES, GOOD FRIENDS, AND LAUGHTER. *YOU* ARE WHAT MAKES THIS DAY SPECIAL, AND YOU DESERVE SO MANY GOOD THINGS.

THIS IS YOUR DAY—ALL YOURS.

# HAPPY BIRTHDAY.

MAY ONLY
# GOOD THINGS
COME YOUR WAY
# EVERY MOMENT
OF TODAY.

UNKNOWN

KNOW THAT

ARE A

OU YOURSELF

MIRACLE...

NORMAN VINCENT PEALE

SHINE LIKE THE WHOLE
UNIVERSE IS YOURS.

RUMI

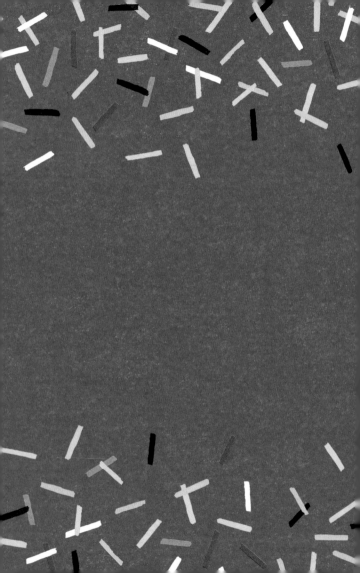

I WISH YOU
ALL THE

# JOY

THAT YOU
CAN WISH.

**WILLIAM SHAKESPEARE**

# LIFE IS WHAT YOU CELEBRATE. ALL OF IT.

JOANNE HARRIS

YOU, WHOSE DAY IT IS,
MAKE IT BEAUTIFUL. GET OUT
YOUR RAINBOW COLORS,
SO IT WILL BE BEAUTIFUL.

TRADITIONAL NOOTKA SONG

# HOW BEAUTIFUL IT IS TO BE ALIVE!

HENRY SEPTIMUS SUTTON

THE BEST AGE IS

# THE AGE YOU ARE.

MAGGIE KUHN

WE TURN
NOT OLDER
WITH YEARS,
BUT NEWER
EVERY DAY.

**EMILY DICKINSON**

MAY LIFE'S GREATEST GIFTS
ALWAYS BE YOURS—HAPPINESS,
MEMORIES, AND DREAMS.

JOSIE BISSETT

A POSSIBILITY WAS BORN
THE DAY YOU WERE
BORN AND IT WILL LIVE AS
LONG AS YOU LIVE.

MARCUS SOLERO

...ON TODAY'S BIRTHDAY, COUNT
YOUR AGE BY FRIENDS—NOT YEARS!

UNKNOWN

ONE
CANNOT
HAVE TOO
LARGE A
PARTY.

JANE AUSTEN

EXPECT THE MOST

# WONDERFUL

THINGS TO HAPPEN...

**EILEEN CADDY**

# MAY YOU BE HAPPY ALWAYS.

HONORÉ DE BALZAC

EVERY SMILE MAKES

'OU A DAY YOUNGER.

CHINESE PROVERB

IT'S GOOD TO
WISH FOR AND LOOK
FORWARD TO THE

# WONDROUS

THINGS IN LIFE.

**MARY SMART**

...HOPE SMILES
FROM THE
THRESHOLD
OF THE YEAR
TO COME...

**ALFRED, LORD TENNYSON**

OPEN YOUR ARMS AS
WIDE AS YOU CAN TO RECEIVE
ALL THE MIRACLES WITH YOUR
NAME ON THEM.

SUZANNA THOMPSON

MAY HAPPINESS
TOUCH YOUR LIFE
TODAY AS WARMLY AS
YOU HAVE TOUCHED
THE LIVES OF OTHERS.

REBECCA FORSYTHE

YOU ARE NOT
ONLY GOOD
YOURSELF, BUT
ALSO THE CAUSE
OF GOODNESS
IN OTHERS.

**SOCRATES**

BE HAPPY FOR THIS MOMENT. THIS MOMENT IS YOUR LIFE.

OMAR KHAYYÁM

NO MATTER HOW OLD YOU ARE,
THERE'S ALWAYS SOMETHING
GOOD TO LOOK FORWARD TO.

LYNN JOHNSTON

THE MORE YOU PRAISE
AND CELEBRATE YOUR
LIFE, THE MORE THERE IS
IN LIFE TO CELEBRATE.

**OPRAH WINFREY**

EVERYONE IS
THE AGE OF THEIR

# HEART.

GUATEMALAN PROVERB

# YOUNG. OLD. JUST WORDS.

GEORGE BURNS

# ADVENTURE LIES AHEAD.

GLENN YARBROUGH

TURN THE WHEEL
OF YOUR LIFE. MAKE
COMPLETE REVOLUTIONS.
CELEBRATE EVERY TURNING.
AND PERSEVERE WITH

JOY.

**DENG MING-DAO**

...YOU PUT SOMETHING

# WONDERFUL

IN THE WORLD THAT
WAS NOT THERE BEFORE.

**EDWIN ELLIOT**

THE BEST IS

# YET TO BE.

ROBERT BROWNING

COMPENDIUM®
live inspired

WITH SPECIAL THANKS TO THE ENTIRE COMPENDIUM FAMILY.

CREDITS:
WRITTEN & COMPILED BY: Kristin Eade
ART DIRECTION BY: Jessica Phoenix
DESIGNED BY: Vanessa Tippmann
EDITED BY: Amelia Riedler & M.H. Clark

ISBN: 978-1-938298-95-0

© 2016 by Compendium, Inc. All rights reserved. No part of
this publication may be reproduced or transmitted in any form
or by any means, electronic or mechanical, including photocopy,
recording, or any storage and retrieval system now known or to
be invented without written permission from the publisher.
Contact: Compendium, Inc., 2100 North Pacific Street, Seattle,
WA 98103. *Happy Birthday*; Compendium; live inspired; and
the format, design, layout, and coloring used in this book are
trademarks and/or trade dress of Compendium, Inc. This book
may be ordered directly from the publisher, but please try your
local bookstore first. Call us at 800.91.IDEAS, or come see our
full line of inspiring products at live-inspired.com.

1st printing. Printed in China with soy inks.